The Occult Sciences

Chiromancy or Palm Reading

By

Various Authors

Palmistry

Palmistry, or 'chiromancy' (from the Greek *kheir* meaning 'hand' and *manteia* meaning 'divination'), is the claim of characterization and foretelling the future through the study of the palm. The practice is found all over the world, with numerous cultural variations, and those who practice chiromancy are generally called palmists, palm readers, hand readers, hand analysts, or chirologists.

Palmistry generally consists of the practice of evaluating a person's character or future life by 'reading' the palm of that person's hand. Various 'lines' (heart line, life line, etc.) and 'mounts' (or bumps), purportedly suggest interpretations by their relative sizes, qualities, and intersections. In some traditions, readers also examine characteristics of the fingers, fingernails, fingerprints, and palmar skin patterns (dermatoglyphics), skin texture and colour, shape of the palm, and flexibility of the hand. A reader usually begins by looking at the person's 'dominant hand' (the hand he or she writes with or uses the most, which is sometimes considered to represent the conscious mind, whereas the other hand is subconscious). In some traditions of palmistry, the other hand is believed to carry hereditary or family traits, or, depending on the palmist's cosmological beliefs, to convey information about past-life or karmic conditions.

Though there are debates on which hand is better to read from, both have their own significance. It is customary to assume that the left hand shows potential in an individual, and the right shows realized personality. The basic framework for 'Classical' palmistry (the most widely taught and practiced tradition) is rooted in Greek mythology. Each area of the palm and fingers is related to a god or goddess, and the features of that area indicate the nature of the corresponding aspect of the subject. For example, the ring finger is associated with the Greek god Apollo; characteristics of the ring finger are tied to the subject's dealings with art, music, aesthetics, fame, wealth, and harmony.

There are three main lines on almost all hands, generally given the most weight by palmists: 'the heart line' (representing love and attraction), 'the head line' (representing the person's mind and the way it works, i.e. learning, intellectualism and communication), and 'the life line' – perhaps the most controversial line on the hand, believed to represent the person's vitality and vigour, physical health and general well being. The life line is also believed to reflect major life changes, including cataclysmic events, physical injuries, and relocations. Contrary to popular belief, modern palmists generally do not believe that the length of a person's life line is tied to the length of a person's existence.

Palmistry has a long history, and is a practice common to many different places on the Eurasian landmass; it has been practised in the cultures of India, Tibet, China, Persia, Sumeria, Ancient Israel and Babylonia. According to some, it had its roots in Hindu Astrology (known in Sanskrit as 'Jyotish'), Chinese Yijing ('I Ching'), and Roma fortune tellers. Several thousand years ago, the Hindu sage Valmiki is thought to have written a book comprising 567 stanzas, the title of which translates in English as *The Teachings of Valmiki Maharshi on Male Palmistry*. From India, the art of palmistry spread to China, Tibet, Egypt, Persia and to other countries in Europe.

From China, palmistry progressed to Greece where Anaxagoras practiced it. Aristotle (384 - 322 BCE) discovered a treatise on the subject of palmistry on an altar of Hermes, which he then presented to Alexander the Great, who took great interest in examining the character of his officers by analyzing the lines on their hands. Aristotle stated that 'Lines are not written into the human hand without reason. They emanate from heavenly influences and man's own individuality.' Accordingly, Aristotle, Hippocrates and Alexander the Great popularized the laws and practice of palmistry. Hippocrates even sought to use palmistry to aid his clinical procedures.

During the Middle Ages the art of palmistry was actively suppressed by the Catholic Church as pagan superstition. In Renaissance magic, palmistry was classified as one of the seven 'forbidden arts', along with necromancy, geomancy, aeromancy, pyromancy, hydromancy, and spatulamancy. It experienced a revival in the modern era however, starting with Captain Casimir Stanislas D'Arpentigny and his publication of *La Chirognomie* in 1839. The 'Chirological Society of Great Britain' was founded in London by Katherine St Hill in 1889 with the stated aim of 'advancing and systematising the art of palmistry and to prevent charlatans from abusing the art.' Edgar de Valcourt-Vermont (Comte de St Germain) founded the 'American Chirological Society' in 1897.

A pivotal figure in the modern palmistry movement was the Irish William John Warner, known by his sobriquet, 'Cheiro'. After studying under gurus in India he set up a palmistry practice in London and enjoyed a wide following of famous clients from around the world, including famous celebrities like Mark Twain, W. T. Stead, Sarah Bernhardt, Mata Hari, Oscar Wilde, Thomas Edison, the Prince of Wales, General Kitchener, William Ewart Gladstone, and Joseph Chamberlain. So popular was Cheiro as a 'Society Palmist' that even those who were not believers in the occult had their hands read by him. The skeptical Mark Twain wrote in Cheiro's visitor's book that he had '...exposed my character to me with humiliating accuracy.'

Criticism of palmistry often rests with the lack of empirical evidence supporting its efficacy. Scientific literature typically regards palmistry as a pseudoscientific or superstitious belief, and skeptics often include palmists on lists of alleged psychics who practice cold reading. Despite this skepticism, palmistry is a practice and branch of human endeavour with an intriguing history – and whether it has any truth or not, provides a fascinating window into folkloric and religious beliefs more generally. We hope the reader enjoys this book on the subject.

CHIROMANCY

I

GENERAL

WE shall in the one word Chiromancy include *chirognomony*, invented by Captain d'Arpentigny, which is morphological physiognomony applied to the hand (therefore dealing only with its outward shape), *chirology*, expression preferred by Mr. Rem and the " scientifics " because it excludes all idea of occultism, and finally *chiromancy* properly so-called, the good old chiromancy which studies in the hand the astral sign-manual, in which Desbarolles believed, that great master of an art which it is possible to modernise without depreciating its ancestors. And we shall keep this word sacred, just because it takes into account occultism without the enlivening of which the science of the hand appears to us incomplete.

The hand is the movement ; the movement is the word ; the word is the soul ; the soul is man. Let us sum up the whole in these words : the soul of man is in his hand. Chiromancy is the art of divining the soul of a person and his fate by examining his hand.

Chiromancy corroborates the astrological and the physiognomonic data. It is easy to see the interest of this triple consultation, each one being like a physician who gives his opinion. An average is struck from these which has a great likelihood of being a precious and definite information from which by deduction it is possible to form a view as to the future of the person interested.

It always remains understood that *free will is able to modify* the natural inclination written in the horoscope, in the features of the face, in the lines of the hand.

But, it will be asked, have these lines really any evidential value. And first of all are they not simply formed by manual work ? In no way, seeing that in the working classes, where they ought to be very marked, they are but slight, and much less marked than in people who lead a more intense intellectual life. Further, they exist in a young child, even in a new born baby who has hardly had time to make many

CHIROMANCY

movements. Further yet, paralysis leads to their disappearance.[1] Therefore let us say it firmly :—The lines of the hand *correspond to the vitality* of the individual. We shall see presently that they also correspond to his temperament and its consequences.

Desbarolles, whom we have just mentioned, with the conscience of a great honest man and his indubitable genius of perspicacity studied for many long years the *physiological problem* presented by these lines. He suggests a scientific explanation of the phenomenon by the animal electricity which is contained in the corpuscles discovered by Pacini which are found in every hand, especially in the palm, the mounts and the tips of the fingers. These reservoirs, he thinks, endow us with an extraordinary sensitiveness which remains in relation with the brain, with all the other senses, with the whole organism. And this would explain why every organic activity is reflected in the hand, and enables us to read in it our physical and mental constitution.

Desbarolles goes farther. He claimed to be able to *foretell* the illnesses with which the client was threatened, because already he saw their germ. . . .[2] And why not ? Why in the same way should not an acute observer be able to foresee, marked in the lines of the palm, the dangerous periods in an existence ?

Thus Chiromancy would be a science more exact even than Physiognomony and than Graphology which anyone sharp enough can lead astray by disguising his handwriting or by looking stern.

. . . . . .

Madame de Thebes, according to Desbarolles, claimed (in 1917) that Chiromancy is in fact a science which has its definite settled and verifiable laws. She wished that a Learned Society should be formed for its close study and to accumulate for this purpose properly checked documents. She denied that there was anything in it which belonged to the Kabbala or to Magic. It is pure Physiology ! she would exclaim, just as anthropology or ethnology. Neither does it in any way, as we have said, fetter our liberty. There is no fatality because there are signs of character and of fate. The will remains entire. Besides, if it is in the left hand that fate is especially written, it is in the right hand that we find possibilities of modifying it.

Born from the civilisations of India and of Egypt, and nursed jointly with Chaldean Astrology, Chiromancy fell into discredit when bunglers and charlatans exploited it without sufficient study and with the sole desire of making money. It is but half a century ago that Desbarolles and d'Arpentigny rescued it from forgetfulness and took it away from the quacks of Divination.

[1] At death the lines disappear little by little, beginning with the slightest.
[2] See on this point farther on the note relating to Mr. Georges Muchery.

THE OCCULT SCIENCES

The hand must be looked upon as a sort of *pentacle*, as a symbol which Nature gives us to decipher. But we must not seek for absolute certainties in it. The obstacle to the spread of Chiromancy lies in the lack of confidence of many, and also in the demands of those who want to know their to-morrows with a precision and with details such as on other subjects they do not ask for a hundredth part from an expert, for instance from a meteorologist or from their doctor !

Let us also remember that the lines of the hand traced at birth under the influence of the stars, are modified as we get older (and not by chance) as the result of changes which take place in our existence or of acts of *will* by which we have thwarted our fate. Chiromancy thus *serves to prove free-will* when reasoning fails !

. . . . . .

We shall see later that we must study not merely the lines of the hand to " make them speak," but also its shape and its movements. A hand meticulously cared for may for instance belong to a vulgar soul which reveals itself by movements resembling it, whilst a coarser and less clear hand may by its noble and frank movements prove that work may injure it without touching (far from it !) the uprightness of him who uses it to earn his bread. Look at an honest labourer and at a courtesan of low degree. The latter from professional necessity, and because she has no more urgent task, will have hands " well made," soft, very clean, adorned with carmined nails ; the hands of the former will be calloused, heavy, the nails still earthy. And yet what a moral difference ! The chiromancer will not make a mistake.

. . . . . .

The Ancients found in the hand the seven reservoirs of astral influence (Desbarolles likened them to a magnetic phenomenon) corresponding to the types of the seven planets which they knew. Thus they had observed that in the Venusians the root of the thumb was always strong and lined ; the Jupiterian had the same sign at the base of the first finger, and so on as to these celestial influences ; they were all revealed at the base of the fingers by a small fleshy protuberance (or if it be absent, by a lined depression). These protuberances are called *the mounts* (mount of Venus, of Jupiter, etc.).

The Ancients had likewise discovered that the fundamental lines of the hand correspond to the construction of our being. It is by numerous and checked observations and notes—how many thousands during so many centuries !—that they have settled—and we carry on their tradition—the correspondence which thus exists between the qualities and abilities of the individual on the one hand, and on the other hand the length, the depth, the colour, the tracing of the lines of the hand.

CHIROMANCY

Therefore we shall be careful in Chiromancy to notice the size of the hand, its general colour, its shape, its temperature, its mounts, its lines and their direction, their strength and their colour, the length and shape of the fingers, the appearance of the nails and the hair, the grain of the skin, and finally particular signs such as squares, circles, stars, dots, crosses, spots, etc., etc.

All these elements are useful. And if, after having applied them, we wish to translate them astrologically, we can with Mr. Jagot classify them in the following manner which will give us an initial typological indication :—

Solar hand :—Elegant, well-proportioned, slightly lemon in colour.
Martian hand :—Massive, fleshy, red.
Selenian (or lunar) hand :—Soft with rounded fingers.
Mercurian hand :—Thin, slender, with pointed fingers.
Venusian hand :—Chubby, pink on white ground, short, with conical fingers.
Jupiterian hand :—Strong, well covered, uniformly deep pink.
Saturnian hand :—Long, bony, thin, dark.
Earthy hand :—Coarse, with square or spatulate fingers.
With, of course, all possible combinations.

But let us go into detail.

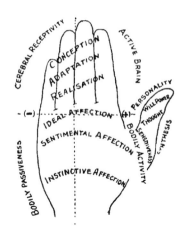

. . . .

On the other hand and without any explanations beyond those given in the table opposite (and it will at once be understood, after reading what precedes and what we have said as to Psycho-Physics) here is the meaning which Mr. Louis Gastin attaches to the hand. His chirological method will easily be seen from it.

II

Outward shape and appearance of the Hand

It is possible to appreciate this *without the knowledge of the persons observed*, and thus to know them a little, without having spoken to them, without having studied their hands, and joining this knowledge

THE OCCULT SCIENCES

to that which is given by their faces, to obtain some support for the distrust or the sympathy with which we enter into relations with them. And here, as farther on, for the sake of clearness and the ease of study, we shall proceed by explanatory tables :—

A.

Well proportioned hand:—General poise in the individual.
Hand too short:—Tendency to bad character.
Hand too long:—Interfering mind, maniacal.
Woman's hand very narrow:—Difficult confinements.
Hand which, at the end of the outstretched arm, touches the knee:—Bad character, fighter, self-willed.
Hand large in comparison with the body:—Smartness, guile.
Hand somewhat long with short fat fingers:—Neglect, laziness, lightheadedness.
Hand fleshy and well articulated:—Long life.
Hand hollow and badly articulated:—Short life.
Hand long, thin, narrow:—Dominative, egotism, unsociability.
Hand short and thin:—Avarice, tendency to gossip.
Hand fat and chubby:—Choice people (if in addition it is well shaped).
Hand badly shaped, twisted:—Bizarre people.
Hand bulging:—Luck, success even without great effort, especially in finance.
Hand soft, pale and swarthy:—Perfidy.
Hand cold, smooth, impassive:—Egotism, lack of sensitiveness.
Hand white, even not reddening in the air: Impenetrability, relentlessness.
Hand supple, a little wrinkled:—Goodness, benevolence, amenity.
Hand hard and wrinkled:—Fighting character.

B.—THE FINGERS.

Fingers well proportioned:—Good character.
Fingers small and thin:—Tendency to eccentricity, to mania.
Fingers well apart:—Egotism, intellect, self-confidence.
Fingers set close together:—Discretion, reasoning power.
Fingers bent back towards the back of the hand:—Smartness, guile.
Fingers separated at the base and meeting at the top:—Omen of misery.
Fingers close together at the base:—Economy, discretion.
Thumb leaning towards the other fingers:—Cynicism, avarice.
Thumb habitually enclosed in the hand:—Nullity of intellect, lack of will-power.
First finger leaning towards the thumb:—Egoistical ambition.
Ring finger longer than first finger:—Intellectual good luck, material bad luck.
First finger longer than ring finger:—Material success, love of pleasure.
Middle finger leaning towards first finger:—Epicurean philosophy.
Middle finger leaning towards ring finger:—Love of advertising, love of arts.
Ring finger leaning towards little finger:—Art taking counsel from science.
Ring finger equal or almost to middle finger:—Love of gambling, of adventure.

CHIROMANCY

C.—THE NAILS.[1]

Nails naturally pink:—Constancy, firmness.
Nails twisted, obtuse:—Independence, rapacity.
Nails pointed at the end of thin fingers:—Weak lungs.
Nails dark and long:—Dangerous people.
Nails short:—Love of fighting and quibbling, irony.
Nails short and hard:—Bad temper, long life.
Nails small, covered with flesh—sensuality.
Nails spotted with white:—Nervousness, happiness.
Nails spotted with black:—Sign of bad luck.
Nails soft:—Weakness, lack of will-power.
Nails breaking:—Weak health.
Nails hard and bent back:—Ambition, spite, passion if they are pointed.
Nails pointed:—Imagination, laziness, love of the arts.
Nails conical:—Feeling for beauty, goodness, truth.
Nails flat, broad, a little curved at the end:—Guile, dissimulation.
Nails grey, pale and round:—Dangerous person.
Nails bitten:—Nervousness, irritability, melancholy (mania called onichophagy)
Nail of little finger defective:—Weak bowels.
Nail of ring finger with quick deformed:—Heart weakness.
Nails " watch glass " shape:—Broncho-pulmonary suppurations.[2]
Nails grooved lengthwise:—Superabundance of nervous fluid.
Nails long:—Timidity, reserve, meticulousness.

D.—COLOUR.[3]

White and transparent:—Indifferent and soft nature.
White and soft:—Lymphatic nature.
Pink with transparent veins:—Benevolence.
Red:—Sanguine complexion, medium health.
Purplish red:—Laziness or bad health.
Swarthy with pink tints:—Good health, good character.
Dark, inclined to greenish yellow:—Bad temper, spite.

A hand should be slightly swarthy, with pink tints, and veins slightly transparent, that is a sign of benevolence, of goodness, of good health (Rem).

---

[1] Are the nails possibly the link between the fluids and the flesh ? Half breeds, even with white skin, for several generations keep the sign of their race in their nails. Balzac says, " The line where our flesh ends and the nail begins, contains the inexplicable and invisible mystery of the constant transformation of our fluids into horn." Are the nails possibly fluid solidified in the air ?

[2] Observation of Dr. P. Marie.

[3] Madame Fraya, the great chiromancer, attaches a particular importance to the colour of the hand. She goes so far as to assert that this colour is affected by the influence of the subconscious before an event, expected or not, takes place which is capable of upsetting destiny.

THE OCCULT SCIENCES

E.—HAIR.

Hand (of a man) without hair :—Effeminate.
Hand normally hairy :—Good complexion, good nature.
Hand hairy on back, calloused in palm :—Heavy and animal mind.
Lower part only hairy :—Great vitality, sign of wit.
Too much hair :—Instability.
Hair scattered :—Temperament lacking order.

Proverb :—*Vir pilosus aut libidinus aut fortis* (a hairy man is amorous or strong). It is told that Condé having been admitted one day, or rather one night, to the house of Ninon de Lenclos and not having given to the famous courtesan sufficient proofs of his amorous prowess, the lady suddenly took his hand, which was very hairy, and exclaimed not without an assumed admiration, " Oh, Monseigneur, how strong you must be ! "

III

Types of Hands

There are four well defined types of hands, according to whether they are pointed (that is to say having all the fingers pointed), square, conical or spatulate. Let us take them one by one.

Pointed hands, that is to say with pointed fingers. " Pointed fingers," says Henri Rem, " offer a conduit free and without obstacle, and in this resemble the magnetised points of lightning conductors ; they easily draw in and emit fluid, consequently absorb spontaneously surrounding ideas and emit them in the same manner. Hence the inspirations, the illuminations, the inventions which flow from pointed fingers and make dreamers, poets and inventors."

To the pointed fingers therefore belong intuitions, arts, ideas, theories, inventions. The pointed hand is the hand of the imaginative, the psychist, the idealist, the aristocrat (or rather the artistocrat, as Gerard de Lacaze-Duthiers would say), the hand of the elect. But alas ! it is not well fitted for the battle of life, for reasoning, for materiality, for effort. Therefore it is also sometimes the hand of laziness, of impulsiveness, of malformation, of exuberance, the hand of luxury, of joy, of charm. It is the hand of the great lovers, the pretty mistresses, the demi-mondaines.

The smooth pointed hand belongs to the poet, the artist, the inventor. If it has philosophical knots (see later), there will be conflict between inspiration and calculation. If material knots are added to it, positive qualities will correct exaggerated idealism.

CHIROMANCY
TYPES OF HANDS

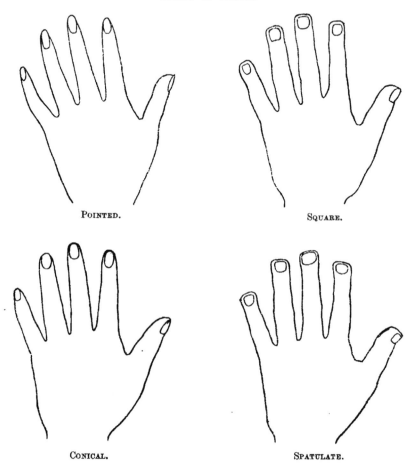

POINTED.   SQUARE.

CONICAL.   SPATULATE.

Henri Rem quotes as examples of the pointed hand:—In politics Robespierre; in painting Raphael, Perugino, Correggio, Antonia de la Gandara and most of the imaginative painters; in literature Milton, Shakespeare, Schiller, Goethe, Chateaubriand, Musset, the elder Dumas, George Sand.

THE OCCULT SCIENCES

Victor Hugo had at first pointed and smooth fingers. Later on they became conical and knotty, the philosophical knot having come up little by little, and the knot of material order having become developed. Alterations of this kind are not rare ; but never in the opposite way will knotted fingers be seen to become smooth, nor spatulate fingers become pointed.

Square hand.—It has the joint with the nail ending in a square by a clear cut. It indicates poise in the character, the taste for meditation, ideas perhaps bourgeois, but in any case firm, clear, well settled. The uncompromising, the intolerant especially have the middle finger very square. The others are at least good philosophers, methodical, cool, thinking and calculating with common sense, executing with order, energy, loving justice, not apt to initiative (the heritage of the pointed finger) but precise, prudent, disciplined, logical in thought, reasoning, deductive. The hand of reason, of duty and of command.

These qualities are strengthened if the fingers have knots at the articulation of the joints. These knots, while in fact not very necessary to the square finger, sign of solid judgment, are the more necessary to the pointed finger whose defects they minimise.

If by an excess of malformation the square finger attains the shape of a ball, a tendency to murder may be feared.

In France more square hands than spatulate hands have been noticed, "that is to say more brains organised for the theory of science than men capable to apply it." The Germans, more able in carrying out, have an abundance of spatulate hands.

Some celebrities with square hands :—

In Politics :—Louis XIV, Vauban, Turenne, Guizot, Fallières, Clémenceau.
In Literature :—Boileau, Voltaire, the younger Dumas, Paul Hervieu.
In Art :—Holbein, Albert Dürer, Le Poussin, Corot, Rodin.
In the Theatre :—Fréderic Lemaître, Rachel, Adelina Patti, Sarah Bernhardt, Got, Leloir, Emma Calvé, Andrée Mégard, Marthe Mellot.

Conical hand.—The hand of reason and of intuition, the philosophical hand *par excellence*. It is partly the square, partly the pointed hand, therefore almost ideal. It is seen in most people of talent if not of genius. It is the hand of him who can understand everything, and love everything, who can acknowledge his errors, be benevolent, friendly, indulgent, the friend of peace and harmony, of order and comfort.

The hand of Molière, La Fontaine, Rousseau, Lamartine, Augier, Mendès, Sully-Prudhomme, Berthelot, Paul Deschanel, Horace Vernet, Delaroche, Meissonnier, Diaz, Gérôme, the brothers Coquelin, Déjazet, Réjane, Berthe Bady, Jane Granier, Arlette Dorgère, Duse, Simone, Robinne, Segond-Weber, Cécile Sorel, Loie Fuller, etc.

CHIROMANCY

Spatulate hand.—Spatula shaped fingers, with the nail joint almost flat (exception must be made in the case of deformation owing to the use of tools).

The hand of instinct, of feelings but little restrained, of the material mind, of revolt (most revolutionaries have these finger signs).

Spatulate fingers belong to the active man who acts before thinking, who is too self-confident, and who is often ruined by his pride.

Those with spatulate fingers are fond of the open air, of daring, of hunting, of travelling, of colonisation, of sailing, or manual work.

They dislike bureaucracy, sedentary occupations, are not much inclined to art and elegance, are gourmand rather than gourmet, artisans rather than artists, lovers of liberty.

A very spatulate thumb indicates quick decision; if the first finger —need for domination, for command; if the middle, love of culture, of construction, in one word of material creation. If the ring finger, it indicates a type meticulous, not very inventive, imitative.

The spatulate hand is resolute rather than resigned. It is often found in Brittany, in the North.

A hard and smooth spatulate hand understands business, is afraid of nothing. If soft, it loses the love of work, but retains that of action (journeys, feasts, walks, etc). On the other hand the influence of the knots (which we shall go into later) may modify it.

Spatulate hands were those of Napoleon III, Lamennais, Fernand Labori, Rubens, Rembrandt, Bouguereau, André Antoine.

Mixed Hand and Elementary Hand.—As will be supposed, there are few hands which can be completely classified into the above pure types. Many are mixed, having fingers of varying kinds, which will in that case keep their particular meaning.

As to the elementary hand, it recalls the earthy planetary type of which we have spoken. It also is earthy and is often found in the country. The fingers are thick, massive, it is the hand of the peasant, instinctive, of the rudimentary being.

This hand abounds in Lapland. It is the helpless hand of the born slave.

. . . . . .

The classification of the hand is not always the same with different chirologists, although in the end they all obtain the same results. By way of example, here is the method adopted by Julien Leclercq in his book, *The Character and the Hand* (published by Juven) :—

We divide, he says, into four classes the hands of people of which we have collected the picture :—

1. Intellectual hands.   2. Brilliant hands.
3. Passionate hands.   4. Practical hands.

THE OCCULT SCIENCES

If we had to draw up a system, we should have to add at least two more classes :—

   5. Vulgar hands.
   6. Insignificant hands.

This division is not theoretical. The method is of the simplest. I confine myself to examining the documents which I have in my hands, and I compare them by taking into account nothing but the sketches which I have before my eyes. And thus I make my groups. Chance will have it that I find four; the exact remembrance which I have of other hands enables me to complete my division.

There remains but one thing to be done—put a label on each group. Here the character, more or less known beforehand, of the personalities in question intervenes together with the chirognomic information gained, and I try to find a common plane, as extensive as possible, on which these personalities may meet.

The description of the various hands and the definition of the corresponding characteristics must be hinted at rather than definite.

The *intellectual hand* is fleshy and half soft, often bony and dry, but never soft or fat. The fingers are strong without being thick at the root, and seem rather long. Their shape is drawn out without being either slim or thin, this being the shape common to this class. It is never short, or even square. Never small, but large or medium. Its parts are balanced, none predominant. The bottom of the hand, which is larger, would not, however, be noticed in relation to the top.

The corresponding *intellectual character* is governed by principles and ideas. It is patient and persevering in its ways. It proceeds after ripe reflection. Not at all or only slightly supple, not be influenced. Methodical and constant work.

The *brilliant hand* is medium or small, never large. The palm is fleshy without being hard, half soft, never bony or dry. This palm is apparently stronger than the fingers which are loose, never thick, rather long. The lower part of this hand, especially towards the mount of Venus, is apt to attract attention. In any case neither thick nor thin. Not square, neither short. It is pretty.

The *brilliant character* is ruled by appearances. It is sociable and malleable. Its instability preserves it from being absorbed. Anxious to attract attention, it prefers rapid methods, schemes and systems being foreign to it ; it is naturally clever and improvises its actions. It proceeds by intuition. Suppleness, assimilation, varied abilities. Work easy but inconstant.

The *passionate hand* is fleshy, resisting, hard, sometimes dry, always strong. The fingers are thick and rather short. It is small, medium or large. If small it seems round ; if large it is apt to be vulgar. It never looks longish. The palm is appreciably broader at the bottom than below the fingers.

The *passionate character* is believing, powerful, active, inspired. It proceeds by a feeling for things and produced by a natural abundance. Capacity for work. Keen, enthusiastic, absorbed worker.

The *practical hand* has a family likeness to the preceding. It is square, but like the passionate hand it is fleshy, often fat. The palm does not appear less broad below the fingers than at the bottom. It is found in all sizes, and when too large it is coarse.

The *practical character* is governed by material needs and by usefulness. It proceeds by reason, produces by interest, obeys calculations, advances with orderliness. It is foreseeing, disdains dreams, repulses illusions. Master of himself, he conforms to circumstances, and is a fighter. Work in proportion to his needs, considerable if necessary. Taste for good living and calm enjoyment.

The *vulgar hand*, of which I could not show an example without hurting someone, is striking by its size and by a suggestion of malformation. It is generally hard and thick. It corresponds to simple tastes.

The *insignificant hand* is too small or too large, very narrow, without resistance, without special features, very soft, with weak bones.

The majority of hands do not belong to a definite type, but it is very rarely impossible to say with some certainty which type prevails.

. . . . . .

By way of example, here are two " famous " hands analysed by J. Leclercq :—

The hand of Father Didon :—The more hands I see, the more it seems to me that they modify my opinions of characters in the sense of greater truth.

I was inclined to believe, some years ago, that Father Didon was a man entirely passionate, vehement, uncontrollable. What a mistake ! He is a brilliant man with a flash of passion. At least that is the view which his hand gave me of him the day when I was allowed to take a photograph of it.

His hand is too small to be a passionate hand, and it is also too pretty. Its relief is prominent and without hardness. The somewhat strong fingers and the prominent places of Venus, Mars and the Moon are its passionate parts.

The little finger is independent, and the thumb, without being long, has power. The will is powerful, without however being so to excess. The fingers are round, almost square—order.

Therefore, if I am to believe this hand, Father Didon adds to his freedom of manner, a greater wish to please than to strike, a quick

THE OCCULT SCIENCES

and assimilable mind, an improvised judgment, a clear intellect and great charm. Add to these gifts colour and intensity.

Self-confidence, indestructible, also belongs to him.

Brilliant men, when they have some degree of passion and are very independent, are not protected, but rather protectors.

In the true passionate character there is always some amount of confusion, of obscurity, but the feelings are deep and the beliefs more solid. The thought of the passionate is slow, it has fetters to break through and roads to force.

The thought is strongly bound to the organism and frees itself with difficulty. In the brilliant type it is like a bubble of air which rises rapidly from the depth of the water to the surface. It is like a strange element, coming from outside, which rapidly finds its way out again.

I do not think that the true passionate has ever been an orator. The latter has too much presence of mind, he does not know disturbance. A flash of passion is enough for him. This is the case with Father Didon.

The hand of Mounet-Sully.—The palm is small in comparison with the fingers. Further, this hand, which has less character than the others, is prettier. Yet it is truly a passionate hand, but with something, some shade, some trace of brilliancy.

Relief prominent, especially around Venus. Fingers strong, flesh fairly firm. Little finger strong and thumb thick. The ring finger is predominant rather than the first finger.

Knowing that this is the hand of an actor, it is possible to say that we are not dealing here with a supple actor, but one who is vehement, playing with his personal feelings, compelled to work hard in order to free his consciousness from a ground in which emotion at first labours confusedly, who does not assimilate easily, who can hardly avail himself of the assistance of others.

A general prejudice is responsible for the belief that the first condition of a remarkable talent is facility. This is an error, for it is not so in the case of basic, personal talents, who depend on themselves for everything.

. . . . . .

We give now, concerning the classification of the types of hands, an entirely new suggestion of G. Muchery [1] which is very interesting because it leads us back to planetary typology.

There are three types of individuals, says this young and already famous chiromancer, the Intellectual, the Passionate and the Material.

The Intellectual derives from Saturn (pride), the Sun (envy) and Mercury (avarice).

---

[1] *Death, Illnesses, Intellect, Heredity, as shown by the imprint of the hand* (published by Astrale, illustrated, 2 volumes, one containing plates).

CHIROMANCY

The Passionate derives from Mars who gives him bad temper, coming from the heart and not the brain.

The Material derives from Jupiter (greediness), Venus (voluptuousness), the Moon (laziness), Earth (materialism).

(It is obvious that these words with apparently bad meaning must be taken in a very broad sense).

The long conical hand is solar.
The short conical hand is lunar.
The long round hand is jupiterian.
The short round hand is venusian.
The long square hand is martian.
The short square hand is earthy.
The long spatulate hand is saturnian.
The short spatulate hand is mercurian.

But pure types do not exist. And besides we are all solar and earthy: the Sun and the Earth are there solely in order to add spirituality or materialism to the other influences.

The type Earth is in reality only a material combination of Mars and Jupiter.

The type Sun in the same way is but a combination of Saturn and Mercury with a touch of Venus.

The Sun gives qualities and defects proceeding from the soul.

The Earth gives qualities and defects proceeding from materialism.

Saturn and Mercury give qualities and defects proceeding from the brain.

Mars gives qualities and defects proceeding from the heart.

Jupiter, Venus and the Moon give qualities and defects proceeding from the body.

From the point of view of colour :—

Generally the Intellectual is yellow, the Passionate red, the Materialist white.
From which we have the following combinations :—

> Colour *dark yellow*—Saturn.
> ,, *light yellow*—Mercury.
> ,, *white-blue*—the Moon.
> ,, *white-yellow*—Venus.
> ,, *white-red*—Jupiter.
> ,, *red*—Mars.

This typology applies to Physiognomony, including Chiromancy. On comparing with this the theories of Jagot, Gastin, etc., we find in fact the same data originally stated by each. On the other hand Mr. Muchery in the book already mentioned states an astro-chiromantic theory which is extraordinarily interesting and to which we refer the reader.

THE OCCULT SCIENCES

IV

The Palm

Apart from the question of lines, we must not neglect the palm, which gives information as to the instincts. In animals the bones of the palm, as a matter of fact, constitute so to speak the whole of the hand ; hence in man predominance of the palm over the fingers indicates a preponderance of animalism. The fingers by their delicacy are the instruments of the soul, the palm is merely the seat of the material, sanguine life. This is seen at once in a sick person in whom it becomes burning as the result of fever. Here the pacinic corpuscles are collected.

A well-coloured, soft, tepid, moist palm indicates youth, good health, sensitiveness. Dry, thin, it shows roughness of character. Over 98·6° the heat is excessive, and (apart from a known illness) this is a sign of weakness of the organism, of bad action of the lungs. Its warmth is also in relation with the blood. The fact that it is cold is however not a proof of the absence of passion. Cold hand, warm heart, says the proverb. And this is not always true either. The line of heart alone gives information as to this. Moist to excess, to some extent perspiring, it denotes a great lymphatic, and also sensuality. If fleshy, it shows a taste for material pleasures. If thin, only the pleasures of the soul are enjoyed. If massive, large, thick and hard with short fingers, it is on the borders of animalism. If simply firm and solid, it is a sign of activity, vigour, vitality. A hard hand is proof of endurance. A soft hand belongs to a temperament of the same kind. A hollow palm foretells lack of courage, even serious illness. A broad palm belongs to the analytical, a long palm to the synthetical, a medium palm to the synoptical, a thin palm to the weak, a palm bare (or almost) of lines to the fatalist, a flat palm without mounts to the neutral, an " agitated " palm, that is to say full of lines, to the passionate of all kinds.

V

The Fingers

The palm is the index to the vital forces. The fingers indicate the intellectual powers. Each of them has its general meaning. Each of them is moreover divided into three *joints,* the unions of which are called *knots.* The first joint (that of the nail) gives information as to the spiritual abilities, the second (middle) as to the intellectual abilities, the third (which is connected with the palm) as to the instincts.

CHIROMANCY

What a fine opportunity this gave to Occultism, and the three parts of the body—the head for mentality, the chest for emotion (sensitiveness), the body for vegetation (nourishment).

We have studied the general shape of the fingers divided into pointed, conical, square, spatulate. Let us now examine each of them more in detail, and for the sake of speed, in the form of tables.

1. THE THUMB

It is the master finger, said Montaigne. It is the thickest, the leader of the file of the others, and can be placed opposite to them. It sums up our vital force, our will. The Ancients looked upon it as the very symbol of man. Cowards had it cut off. In Sparta, the teachers as a punishment bit the thumbs of their lazy pupils. In the Circus it was with the thumb, turned up or down, that the Emperor condemned or spared the vanquished. The thumb is man, wrote d'Arpentigny. Idiots have a short thumb without any corpuscles at all, as has been demonstrated by Dupuytren. The new-born baby, as yet without will-power, holds its thumb hidden in its closed hand; the epileptic, who has lost his will-power, does the same, as also the patient who is grievously ill, the paralytic, the dying. The joints of the thumb represent: the first energy, the second logic, the third affection.

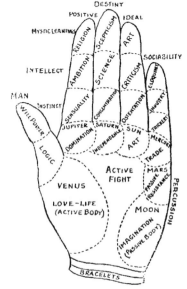

THE FINGERS AND THE MOUNTS OF THE HAND.

We may therefore draw up the following table :—

First joint too long—pride, obstinacy.
First joint long and strong—strong will-power.
First joint short—indecision, self-distrust, weakness (unless it is broad).
First joint very short—passivity.
First joint broad, strong, swollen—stubbornness (for instance Proudhon).
First joint ball-shaped—pigheadedness, even brutishness.
First joint pointed—poetic sensitiveness (Victor Hugo).
First joint conical or round—varied but slight abilities.
First joint square—practical and reasoned will-power.
First joint spatulate—impulsive will-power.

THE OCCULT SCIENCES

Second joint long and strong—justice, clarity, logic.
Second joint depressed or short—lack of judgment.
Third joint (root of the thumb—see Mount of Venus).

But it is not enough to consider the joints by themselves. Their relations amongst each other are also of value. For instance :—

The two first joints equal—good balance (F. de Lesseps).
First thick and long, second short—energy without logic.
First short, second long—more logic than will-power.

The debauched and prostitutes often have the root of the thumb developed and the remaining two joints short.

According to d'Arpentigny :—

Thumb short—more feelings than ideas ; more heart than reason and energy.
Thumb long—the head predominates, will-power, personality, firmness, perseverance.
Thumb very long—dominating will-power of the leaders, the ambitious, the arrivists.[1]
Thumb thin—organic weakness.
Thumb narrow—guile and subtlety.
Thumb thick—solid temperament.

Distrust the thumb which is bent back (cowardice). Choose your servants among the short thumbs. A thumb not very loose indicates frankness and disdain of prejudices. Desbarolles claims that he has several times seen the sign of eroticism in a hand where the thumb, in the middle of the palm, may take a kind of phallic shape (as in the case of the murderer Castex, etc). Avoid persons who have the habit of enclosing their thumb in their hand, and thus suppress their own will-power.

2. THE FIRST FINGER

It is the finger which points, orders, threatens, decides, attacks. It is the finger of Jupiter.

Pointed—contradicts its role. Tendency to contemplation leanings to art.
Conical—it is said that in this case it predisposes to reading and gentle simplicity.
Square—bourgeois, orderly, regular leanings.
Spatulate (rare)—exaggerated mysticism.
Straight, upright—love of independence and fighting (the Irish patriot Maud Gonne).
Short—tempered ambition (unless it is hard, thick, spatulate).

[1] Many great men had large thumbs—Descartes, Newton, Galileo, Leibnitz, Danton, Luther, Corot. Voltaire had enormous thumbs. Montaigne, La Fontaine had the nail joint of the thumb rather short, because they were ruled by doubt or by a naiveté which formed the charm of their genius.

CHIROMANCY

As in the thumb, let us rapidly study the joints :—

First, long—intuition, religiousness.
First, short—scepticism, unbelief (especially if it is square).
First, fleshy—sensual pleasures.
First, dry—stern religion.
First, broad, with nail bent back—phthisis and scrofula (medical observation).
Second, long—ambition determined to succeed.
Second, short—efforts without success.
Second, dry—ambition, love of glory.
Third, long, strong—love of domination.
Third, short—retirement.
Third, dry—disdain of the joys of life, asceticism.

3. THE MIDDLE FINGER

The finger of the centre. The axis of life. Represents destiny. Besides derives from the Mount of Saturn.

Pointed—loses its saturnian character. Intuition. Study of great problems easy.
Square—rigour, intolerance, discipline.
Spatulate, flat topped, swollen—sombre sadness, taste for profound studies love of the soil and of mines.
Long—gloomy pride, doubt of self, fatalism.
Thick—philosophical materialism.
Nail joint long, broad—prudence, morbidness.
Nail joint short—gentle resignation.
Nail joint thin, dry—scepticism and funereal simplicity.
Second joint long—love of agriculture, and, with knot, of occultism.
Second joint short—uselessness of all experience of life.
Third long—avarice, love of mortification.
Short—well thought out economy.

4. THE RING FINGER

Finger of the sun, of the ring In sympathy with the heart. Finger of art and the ideal.

Pointed—fortunate æsthetic leanings.
Conical—more disposed to commerce.
Square—love of riches, of artistic truth found in reason.
Spatulate—art applied to movement (painting of battles, military marches, the dance, the theatre).
Short—indifference to glory, and if very short, low instincts.
Long—love of show, of spending, of fame.
Knotty—reasoned love of beauty.
Badly shaped—shameful celebrity (of criminals).

THE OCCULT SCIENCES

First joint long—noble love of art, of intellectual asceticism (less noble if it is short).
First joint fleshy—definite and sensual seeking after beauty.
First joint dry—spiritual seeking after beauty.
Second long—reason in art, talent, originality.
Second short—impossibility of success (the failures).
Second fleshy—realistic art.
Second dry—idealistic art.
Third—long in proportion to the probability of success.

5. THE LITTLE FINGER

The chattering finger. The mercurian finger of skill, of intuition, of eloquence, of nous.

Pointed or conical—natural eloquence, perspicacity.
Square or spatulate—practical and reasoned science, physical skill.
Short—quick assimilation.
Long—reflection, knowledge of life, perfectibility.
Knotty—pronounced commercial abilities.
Badly shaped—bad luck, lack of skill.
Folded inward—sign of arthriticism (according to Professor Landouzy).
First joint long—taste for study.
First joint short—mental laziness.
Second—short or long according to cleverness in speculation.
Third—long or short according to guile or simplicity.

Sometimes the little finger has, or seems to have, only two joints. If the nail joint is the longer—lack of guile and intellectual qualities. If it is the shorter—the practical sense dominates the æsthetic sense.

VI

The Knots

The knots are the prominant articulations which connect the joints.
The knot called philosophical binds the nail joint to the second.
The knot called material binds the second joint to the third.
Smooth fingers may become knotty. The contrary never occurs.
Exaggerated knots denote excess, hence disorder of the faculties.
The philosophic knot is the index of the need to know, to compare, to discuss, sometimes to deprecate others, to doubt everything. Few women have it. Desbarolles says that it is often seen among Parisians, as well as the square finger and the smooth finger.

CHIROMANCY

The knot of material order denotes the practical qualities, the love of order, of well-being, of wealth. It is useful for commercial men, business men, calculators.

If these two kinds of knot exist, they spoil the beauty of the hand, but are a benefit to the possessor. Knots are useful to pointed or spatulate hands. They give reflection and patience.

VII

The Handshake

According to the Daguesah, this also gives information. It has been possible to draw up the following little table as to this :

Ordinary with good-nature :—Superficial or cunning men.
Short :—Men avaricious or afraid of emotion.
Dragging :—The simple formality of the indifferent.
Brutal :—That of a bully or a rude man.
Broad and frank :—Of a friend, a good-hearted man.
Heavy :—Of the indolent to whom all movement is a task.
From the tips of the fingers :—Of the disdainful (insolent gesture).
Caressing and lasting :—Of a voluptuary.
Caressing with pressure :—Carnal desire.

VIII

The Mounts

However much the " scientific chirologists " disclaim their interest in Astrology, they are compelled to admit that the protuberances at the roots of the fingers and at the percussion (the outer part of the hand opposite to the thumb which is used when banging with the fist) are the synthesis of the abilities and instincts given to each of these fingers. At these points there are heaps of pacinic corpuscles which are as it were the condensers of the nerves of the hand, reservoirs of magnetic electricity, of rising sap. Perhaps it is not foolish to think that the *astral sign-manual* is there, and explains, together with the names which the scientifics have had to preserve, the corresponding planetary influence.

However this may be, here is the list and the place[1] of these protuberances :—

At the root of the thumb :—The mount of Venus.
At the root of the first finger :—The mount of Jupiter.

---

[1] See p. 163: the drawing of the fingers and the mounts of the hand.

THE OCCULT SCIENCES

At the root of the middle finger :—The mount of Saturn.
At the root of the ring finger :—The mount of the Sun.
At the root of the little finger :—The mount of Mercury.
Below the mount of Mercury :—The mount of Mars.
Below the mount of Mars :—The mount of the Moon.
Between these seven mounts, the remaining space is called the Plain of Mars.

Pre-eminent mounts always denote an abundance, even a plethora of fluid. When flat, they denote a relative absence of power, of sap, of passion. When hollow, they show the contrary of the abilities indicated.

Lines on the mounts indicate increased nervous power. One mount larger than all the others shows the dominant influence on the life. If it is distinguished beyond all others, this excess is probably rather fatal, a real tyranny exercised over the person.

Let us now consider each of these little mounts, so remarkable and so expressive.

1. MOUNT OF JUPITER

Below the first finger, and like it, it refers to ambition, to dominance, to honours.

Well proportioned, it gives the jupiterian qualities of reward well earned, of the joy of living, of normal recompense. It foretells happy marriages, loving unions.

In excess :—Pride, the desire to shine, to command, exaltation, superstition.
Depressed :—Lack of dignity, common leanings.
Leaning towards the mount of Saturn :—Religious aspirations. *If it absorbs the latter :*—Success at any price.

If there are to be seen :—

Straight upward lines :—Good prospect of success.
Cross lines :—Domestic sorrows (Victor Hugo had this fatidic sign ; his terrible losses are well known).
Dots :—Position in danger, disappointed ambition.
A bar :—Delayed opportunities.
A triangle :—Aptitude for diplomatic sciences.
A cross :—Happy omen of love.
A star :—The best of all signs. Complete satisfaction. This sign never lies (Rem).

2. MOUNT OF SATURN

Below the middle finger and its symbol of destiny.
Plain, full, smooth—quiet life :—Possible success if other unlucky signs are absent.

CHIROMANCY

Pre-eminent (rare) :—Serious, bitter, splenetic character.
Leaning towards Jupiter :—Ambition is victorious over science. Bad reputation.
Leaning towards the Sun :—Artistic tastes, but leaning towards melancholy.
One or more dots on it :—Fatality, unhappiness.
A triangle :—Aptitude to mystical or occult sciences.
A cross :—Fatal mysticism.
A star :—Threat of serious illness, paralysis, painful death, murder.

3. MOUNT OF THE SUN

Below the ring finger—glory, wealth, artistic leanings. Therefore if normal it is a good sign. If excessive, it draws beyond these noble qualities to their opposite defects. Depressed it cancels these tendencies.

Slight and plain :—Quiet life, without fame.
Ascending lines :—Are as usual signs of good prospects.
Disordered lines :—Exuberance, presumption, lightheartedness.
Cross lines :—Struggles, obstacles, changes.
A star :—Possibly dangerous successes (e.g. General Boulanger).
A bar :—Vanity, false glory, lack of power, hindrances.
A triangle :—Great artistic aptitudes.
A small island at the bottom and on the line of the Sun :—Success, perhaps as the result of adultery.
Holes or pits :—Diseases of the kidneys.

4. MOUNT OF MERCURY

Below the little finger. Intelligence, abilities, eloquence, medicine, commerce.

Normal :—Possibility of success in the Mercurian branches of activity.
Abnormal :—Theft, cunning, lies, bankruptcy, discredit, pretentious ignorance.
Depressed or absent :—None of the abilities resulting from the mount.
Swollen, leaning towards the percussion :—Extreme cunning, greed for gain.
Leaning towards the Sun :—Union of art to eloquence and to science.

It has been observed that people with leanings towards medical or natural sciences, the wives, daughters or mistresses of doctors, nurses, hospital sisters, etc., have on Mercury rising lines. If at the same time the mount of the Moon is strongly developed they take care of themselves and drug much. They are the type of the imaginary patient.

Unions, marriages, widowhoods, children, are written on the percussion of the mount of Mercury.

Cross or bar on this mount :—Kleptomania (leaning to theft).
Triangle :—Diplomatic or political abilities.

THE OCCULT SCIENCES

5. MOUNT OF MARS

It represents struggle, resistance. Normal it gives courage, calm, self-restraint. Even its excess is favourable, especially if the thumb is large (will-power). Big and plain it indicates firmness, tenacity. Absent or flat, the contrary—flabby, cowardly beings without character. United with the Moon in one single swelling, it betokens resigned heedlessness.

On Mars lines are a bad sign; they make violent, foretell bronchitis, laryngitis. A star threatens a serious wound (many had it who died in the war). A bar means possible violent death. A triangle—military science.

The plain of Mars often contains the signs of the struggles of life. Smooth, without wrinkles, it means peace. Hollow, it means non-resistance. With many lines, it indicates constant fighting. But the fighting often comes from the Martian himself; a cross on the plain shows him violent and quarrelsome. If in addition the head line is short, then all the wild passions are let loose. A triangle there promises military glory. A large cross united to a Venus line leads to the date of a catastrophe; as witness the Empress Eugenie who with this sign bore the prediction of the Franco-German war for about her forty-fifth year; in it she lost her crown and soon after her husband.

6. MOUNT OF THE MOON

If normal it gives, according to Desbarolles, a gentle melancholy and poetic imagination, love of dreaming and of silence, of harmony and mystery. But if exaggerated, the caprices of the Madwoman of the House, mobility, sadness, fanaticism, vapours and megrims.

If absent or depressed, no sense of beauty, of enthusiasm, of illusion, but a cold, dry, hard character. If thin and lined, it betokens lascivious curiosity. Striated, it is a sign of madness, of irritation, of effervescence, of the dread of chimæras, of the love of the odd. These troubles come from the heart if that line is predominant, from pride with a strong jupiterian mount, from business with a prominent Mercury, from love if Venus is mistress.

Lunar lines incline to forebodings, to premonitory dreams, to hallucinations. Together with large eyes and a good head line, good memory and aptness for languages are foretold. A star on the Moon mount foretells a danger on the water, and poor Lantelme who died drowned, had it, very strongly marked on a line of travel on the percussion of the hand. An island on the mount makes the somnambulist, the seer, gives the divining sense (e.g., the younger Dumas). A triangle means common sense, intuition, maritime science; a bar sorrow, restlessness, exaltation, in the woman shamelessness. On the percussion

CHIROMANCY

are found imagination (more or less numerous small lines) and journeys (horizontal lines going towards the back of the hand).

7. MOUNT OF VENUS

It is the root of the thumb, the largest of the mounts of the hand. The line of life surrounds it. It is the seat not so much of love as of vital essence, the movements of the soul, affectibility, attractions towards joy and voluptuousness.

Nevertheless if sentimental love is especially written on the heart line, it is on the mount of Venus that sensual love is inscribed. If therefore it is harmonious, normally striated, the pleasures of the senses will attract normally, and also the intellectual pleasures, music, the dance, beauty, luxury. If it is weak and smooth—small attraction to lust. On the contrary the latter is victorious together with its unhappy train on an exaggerated lined mount, especially if thick and hard. The true libertine, says Desbarolles, is shewn by the manifold lines which are accentuated by a ring of Venus (see below). Most of the gallant women have this, together with a short thumb (lack of will-power). But a curious thing is that persons with the same sign, if they have a pointed first finger, may also incline towards mysticism, in their troubled need to love something—the flesh or a God.

Sometimes we see on the mount of Venus dots, signs of accidents; a triangle, sign of base calculation in love; a bar, sign of lasciviousness, of sexual perversion; a cross, sign of a sole and unhappy love (unless a further cross, on Jupiter, transforms this unhappiness into happiness); a star, possible sign of unhappiness in love (if the star is connected with the head line, divorce or separation).

It is said that four equidistant lines going from the root of the thumb to the mount of Venus denote inheritances at a ripe age (Rem); that if these lines are placed towards the end of the life line it means that the legacy will come in youth; that if there are only two or three it means that the legacy will not be so considerable; finally that if these lines cross each other at the end, it means a lawsuit on this matter. It is said that several lines crossing on the top of the mount of Venus towards the jointure of the thumb mean fall from a horse, from a vehicle, or accident in the mountains. It is said that the root of the thumb cut in several places foretells death by drowning or by strangling, that one or two thick lines crossing the thumb threaten murder or beheading. But let us leave these funereal presages and come to more cheerful ones:
—numerous and rather shallow small lines tell of little love affairs; not very numerous thick lines proclaim the serious passions; lines going from the root of the thumb to the life line and meeting on the mount reveal a double love.

THE OCCULT SCIENCES

IX

The Lines of the Hand

These are the great revealers, the pythonesses who are most easily questioned and who reply most obediently. They are the varying signs of vitality, of energy, of sensitiveness, which the astral influence signed from the day of birth. Their decrees modify those of the mounts and the fingers. They reflect the will of the brain, its impulses, its starts, its weaknesses, even its organic blemishes, and the whole of the past, present and future existence of the subject. They in some way automatically record our deeds, and even forewarn us, they tell us mutely of our fate.[1]

The lines of the hand, at least the chief ones, are formed in the maternal womb, at the same time as the features of the face. " God placed signs in the hands of men," say the Sacred Books, " so that all might know their fate." These lines change during the course of life and disappear at death.

The diversity of temperaments and of vitalities causes their variety. There are no two persons with the same lines. The lines are the more numerous according to whether we have a complicated or sensitive soul. The working classes have much more simple lines than men and women of the world or the elect. They change, we repeat, under the influence of our occupations and preoccupations.

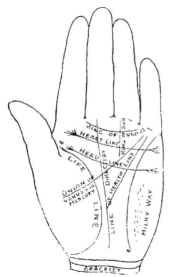

THE LINES OF THE HAND.

Each hand corresponds to the opposite brain, the right to the left hemisphere, the left to the right hemisphere, as is proved by hemiplegia.

---

[1] " Troubles, sorrows, the great moral shocks, reverses of fortunes, illnesses, accidents, leave traces on the face, on the physiognomy, engrave lines on it which even change its features and its expression. These events of a life, these revealing reflexes, inscribe themselves by corresponding stigmata on the hand as on the face. It is the same with all important events, with accidents to beware of, with morbid germs which must open and blossom at a more or less early time. The date of the event and that of the blossoming inscribe themselves also in the hand. Violent impressions, even if received in childhood, produce and leave their stigmata and their trace in the hand." (Henri Rem, *op. cit.* p. 158).

CHIROMANCY

The number of the lines of the hand is considerable. They may be divided into :—

Three principal ones (lines of life, head, heart).
Four secondary ones (lines of fate, sun, health, intuition).
Eleven ancillary ones, of which the rings round the wrist, the ring of Venus etc., are described later.

Let us give a few general remarks on the lines.

The principal and secondary lines are sometimes accompanied by a sister-line which mends their bad effect in case of breaks, but increases this bad effect if the line itself is not good, or doubles the good effect if both are good.

The colours of the lines must be considered. Pale or light yellow they betoken lymphaticism, therefore calm. Red they are a sign of sanguineness, therefore of power, of passion, even of violence. Yellow they are a sign of bile, hence of pessimism, of sadness. Livid, dark blue, they show materialism, disorder, grudge, especially if the fingers corroborate these defects.

Good lines, that is to say those which are complete, clear, fairly broad and deep, are a sign of good character, of normal fate ; their predictions in this case are very sure.

Imperfect lines, confused, twisted, denote a bizarre being, lacunæ, dangers. If too strong, this sign is excessive. Very deep they intensify it. Fine and numerous they mean nervousness, activity. Broad, not very deep, not very numerous, they show calm and power of resistance. Broken, cut, they mean stops, changes, dangers, restless fate. Regular and numerous they indicate a noble life, intellect, sensitiveness.

These lines and signs are not the same in the two hands which supplement each other. If the two hands are appreciably alike, their predictions are the surer. If not, they must both be looked at, remembering that the right hand is that of activity, the left that of passivity. The hand which has the greater number of lines is the dominant of the subject, that is to say shows whether he is more active or passive. The man of feeling will have the left hand more lined. He will have the luck of chance. He whose right hand is more lined has only himself to rely upon.

Apart from the lines, the hand contains various signs, stars, crosses, triangles, bars, isles, chains, etc., which we shall look at in the following pages.

. . . . . .

The Line of Life.—It is the one which runs like a rivulet of sap round the vast promontory of Venus. It is the most important, the one which indicates the amount of vital energy, the probabilities of long life, of serious accidents. We must therefore study it carefully.

THE OCCULT SCIENCES

The writer of our introduction has already observed that, according to the opinion of Fraya, it would be better to name it the line of vitality, for its length is not, as the man in the street (or the sibyl of low degree) generally claims, necessarily in accord with the number of years we have to live. If it were, it would be criminal or at least dangerous to tell the client exactly his early or distant end, thus implanting in him a fixed idea which would be capable, as the fatal hour approached, of putting him into such a state of moral and physical inferiority that he would run the risk of himself advancing the hour of his death. In the same way the client, by taking the necessary care of his health, is able to strengthen it and thus himself to *lengthen* this line which, we repeat, is but a sign of vitality. On the other hand, and this is remarkable, a line of life will never shrink from the length which it shows at the moment of examination. If for instance it indicates that a person aged 50 may *possibly* live to 70, it may be that he will live even to 80, but he will not live only to 60 except in the case of a sudden accident, which anyhow would also be written in the palm.

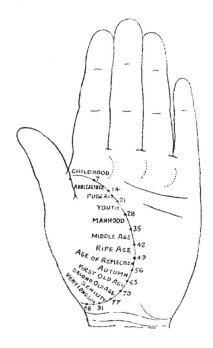

However this may be it is possible roughly to say that when the line of life reaches to the line round the wrist, there is the *possibility* that it will mark at least 80 years on the dial of life. By dividing the line from its start below the mount of Jupiter, up to this point either by ten or by seven years, [1] we obtain a scale of the stages of life as follows:

From birth to 7 years, which is the age of reason (childhood). Instincts, probable character.

From 7 to 14 years, which is the " difficult age " (adolescence). Natural aptitudes.

[1] The traditionalists made this division by ten. The " renovators " of chiromancy make it by 7, basing themselves on the doctrine of the physiologist Flourens who teaches that the total renewal of the cells of the body takes place in 7 years. We have adopted this latter method which admits of a more rational division of the " ages " of life. And who does not see that here we adopt once more the occult law of the septenary ?

CHIROMANCY

From 14 to 21 years (that is to say the time of puberty). Illusions and hopes.

From 21 to 28 years, the period of sensual pleasures (youth). Physical love, enthusiasms, inconstancy.

From 28 to 35 years (manly age). Physical and intellectual pleasures. The best time of life.

From 35 to 42 years (middle age). Consistent desire for wealth or honour.

From 42 to 49 years (ripe age). Wisdom, reason, culminating point of life.

From 49 to 56 years (critical age). Prudence, foresight, care of the health so as to " round the cape."

From 56 to 63 years (autumn). Reflections and first regrets.

From 63 to 70 years (first old age). Infirmities, pains, trouble or quiet in the home.

From 70 to 77 years (second old age). The fingers become knotty, the heart also. The character is apt to become bitter.

From 77 to 84 or 91 years (senility). Distrust, the grave yawns.

After the age of 91, if man still lives, he becomes again a child, indifferent, vegetating, inert, ghostly.

In order to classify events according to their dates, the scale of the stages of life will therefore be consulted. We now give a table of the chief peculiarities of the line of life :—

Good line, long, pink, free of signs, or breaks—good and long life.

Pale and not very broad—delicate health, lymphaticism.

Pale and broad—little strength in much sap. Very broad—bad health (valetudinarianism).

Red—strong health; red and broad—violence; livid and very broad—spitefulness, brutality.

Bluish—venusian character. Dark blue—martian character (bad temper).

Long—possibility of long life. Long and thin—but little sap, timidity, nerves.

Like a chain, broken—sickly and troubled life.

Broken at birth—illness in early childhood.[1] Often interrupted—many illnesses.

Tortuous—unequal temper. Badly drawn—delicate but resisting health.

Short—risk of short life (especially if the two hands are alike).

In two pieces—mortal danger (unless in the other hand the line is not cut).

Double—great vital power. In women the sign of passion without

[1] Broken in one hand, continuous in the other indicates the *certainty* of an illness which has placed or will place in danger of death (Desbarolles).

restraint (e.g. Clara Ward, who married a prince, then the Gipsy Rigo, then the undistinguished Italian Ricciardo, and lower still a man named Cassalota). Victor Hugo had the rarity of a triple life line. His enormous vitality is well known.

Branches at the start—promise of wealth. At the end, towards Venus—loss of fortune; towards the ring round the wrist—misery.

Branches thrown out from the corner of the life line towards the head line—success. Towards the Moon—rheumatism. Towards the plain of Mars—full success but after trials. Towards Saturn or the Sun—fame, wealth.

A line at the start going towards Jupiter—ambition, success.[1]

Life line forked towards the bottom—weakening on the turn of life. Rest necessary when the time comes (Lamartine had this mark, to which we owe a fine melancholy page written by Arsène Houssaye).

Clean lines proceeding from the life line—success due to personal merit.

Straight line going to Venus or from the life line to Mercury—successes in business or in love.

Lines crossing the life, head or heart line—changes of position, of fortune or of fate.

Lines going from Venus to the plain of Mars, called lines of sorrow—illness, bad luck.

. . . . . .

The Line of Head.—It is found in the middle of the hand, starts between the thumb and the first finger, forms with the life line " the supreme angle," and traversing the plain of Mars, ends by the percussion. It is the line of mental activity. On it are inscribed wounds of the head, neurasthenia, madness, all the mental diseases, and also qualities of initiative and reasoning. Its absence in a hand is a sign of death by accident.

In order to ascertain the approximate date of the events foretold by it, it is divided by perpendicular lines drawn on to it from the middle of each finger, from the first finger to the little finger, which gives five divisions, from 0 to 10 years, from 10 to 15, from 15 to 25, from 25 to 50 and from 50 to 75.

If clear, long, straight, slightly sloping, it indicates balance of faculties and firm will-power.

If very long, going to the percussion, straight, dry, it means excessive reasoning, therefore some egoism, positivism, calculation in everything, arrivism, self-restraint. It was like this in Corot's hand, and no doubt in Fontenelle's to whom Tensin said that he had a brain instead of a heart. If in addition such a line curves towards Mercury or sends a

[1] It sometimes comes up suddenly before a future success (Rem).

CHIROMANCY

branch in that direction, it means that calculation turns to cunning, to a genius for affairs even somewhat unscrupulous.

When it is forked and one branch goes towards the Moon, it indicates an aptitude to invent opportune lies (sophists, advocates, solicitors, and also actors who drop their own personality at will so as to represent their part, and women who are clever at getting out of difficulties).

If the line plainly slopes towards the mount of the Moon, it means a leaning towards imagination, towards poetry. If it is goes lower down, it means taste for simplicity, for occultism, for spiritualism.

If double, the head line foretells probability of money in middle life.

If it leaves the life line late, it is a sign of late development of the intellect. If it begins without touching the life line it indicates serious eye trouble in youth. If starting beneath the middle finger, the development of the intellect is considerably hindered.

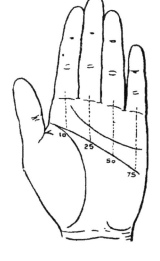

If short, the character is weak. Ending beneath the middle finger shews danger of death in youth. Stopping below the ring finger means in women coquetry, in men unfaithfulness, often a spoilt life.

Cut near the start—wounds or disease of the lower limbs, wounds to the head generally as the result of a fall.

Cut in pieces—tendency to headaches, lack of memory or stupidity. If in two pieces—serious wound or madness. If the pieces cross each other under Saturn—severe accident (it is found in many criminals condemned to execution).

Will-power, courage are in proportion to its depth. If thin and feeble—lassitude, lymphaticism.

Pale and broad it indicates mental inactivity; red, energy; too red, danger of apoplexy or epilepsy.

Ascending and curved is a bad sign—a great misfortune threatens life.

Tortuous it means liver trouble, spite, lies, inconstant will.

Badly formed, confused, scattered—weakness of the brain, madness, illnesses.

Inclined towards the life line—certain happiness. Near to the heart line—palpitations, asthma, suffocation. Rising and joining the heart line—the heart governs the head. But if a branch goes towards the heart line, it is on the contrary the head which governs the heart. A branch towards Jupiter and ending on a star means great success; but without a star and rising towards the first finger, simple pride.

The Line of Heart.—It runs from the first finger to the percussion, at the base of the mounts. It is the voice of the joys and the sorrows of life, of emotion, of heart troubles, more eloquent in women and more explanatory in them than in men. Its oracles are supplemented by the study of the mount of Venus and by the little lines of passion of which we shall speak presently.

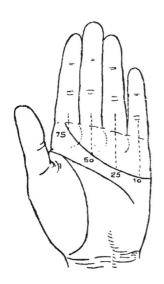

The heart line is divided, like the head line, by straight lines drawn from the middle of the fingers starting with the little finger, but counting is in the reverse direction, 10 (years) being below the little finger, and 25, 50 and 75 below the others.

A good heart line, without accidents, well coloured, straight, normally deep foretells a normal love, made up of serious affection, goodness, conjugal happiness, sane friendships, a well balanced soul. It is generally like this in French women of all social classes; it is found in the heroines of the Revolution:—Madame Tallien, Madame de Mouchy, Madame Roland, Mlle. de Sombreuil, Madame de Rosambo who on meeting the latter when going to the scaffold said to her: "You have had the happiness of saving your father, I have the consolation of dying with mine." According to Rem it is found in true and sympathetic orators, earnest lawyers, great preachers, great dramatic artists.

A very large line, especially with branches at the two ends, shows an excess of sensitiveness. Those of Lamartine, of Sully-Prudhomme, were of this kind.

Pale, it denotes more calm, and red, an ardour which sometimes turns to violence.

Slight, thin, fine, it means dryness. Too hollow, cruelty (parricides). Double, great expansiveness (Dejazet).

A large line, if the mount of the Moon is striated, betokens jealousy, which is also shewn by the ring of Venus.

If beginning in the first finger—wealth; if under Jupiter, idealism; in both cases honours and riches are possible. On the contrary mis-

CHIROMANCY

fortune and loss of property is foretold if the line starts at the root of the first finger; hard work and luck if it starts between the first and middle fingers; troubled life if it begins under the middle finger; poverty of heart and of mind if it starts under the ring finger.

If stopping under the middle finger, danger of short life; if under the ring finger, conceit; if under the little finger, cleverness rather than sincere love.

Sloping towards the head line—hypocrisy or domination of the heart by the head. Joining it under the middle finger, risk of violent death. According to Rem, if it slopes towards and joins the head line and the life line and forms a St. Andrew's cross on the mount of Jupiter it indicates a union or a marriage entailing suffering and loss of money.

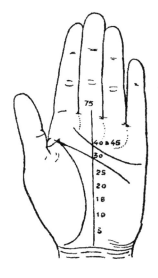

A confused chain-like heart line indicates moral prodigality of the heart, physically a tendency to palpitations. This is the case with those who are picturesquely called "artichoke hearts." If tortuous at the ends—heart trouble. Cut or intersected by other lines—inconstancy. Forked, bad circulation.

Throwing at the start a branch towards Jupiter—strong and tender passion; three branches, wealth.

. . . . . .

Some authors place the line of Fate among the principal, others among the secondary lines. It does not matter. We will now deal with it, and with three other lines, those of the sun, of health and of intuition.

The Line of Fate.—Also called the line of luck, of fortune, of fatality, or saturnian. It is the one which starts from the ring round the wrist (or from the life line or from the plain or the mount of Mars or the mount of the Moon) and which ends at the middle finger. The Ancients called it the line of fate or of fortune, but gave to these words their etymological meaning—that which happens, that which comes. It must therefore not be translated in the sense that the line denotes " good luck " or wealth. In our opinion, which we offer to chiromancers, it must be considered as indicating the *realisation* or otherwise of the individual in accordance with his abilities. It can therefore be good

THE OCCULT SCIENCES

in a peasant, a rich man, a poor man, a man of small position, a nobleman, a maidservant, a priest, etc., if they have " realised " their lives according to their respective abilities.

It is a curious line, changeable even during the course of life, rich in combinations. Its direction towards one mount or the other denotes the tendency of the powers of the individual—here towards the arts, there towards position, elsewhere towards commerce. Those in whom it is absent or weak may possibly succeed, but they have only themselves to rely upon.

In order to know the approximate dates of the events, it is divided like the others, by placing 30 (years) where it crosses the head line, and normally 15 at the end, by the mount of Saturn.

If good in both hands it means assured success.

If better at the beginning than at the end, hard times in old age.

If irregular in a hand with many lines—excessive sensitiveness making success difficult.

Accompanied by small lines—good omen, obstacles overcome.

Made up of small lines—illnesses, indecision.

Confused—changeable fate, capricious; also if it is broken, cut, reconnecting at each instant.

If it has ascending branches—destiny improves little by little (towards the sign of the mount attained).

Its beginnings are important. If at the ring round the wrist, and straight to the end—happy calm fate. If at the life line, happiness acquired by merit. At the mount of Mars—power of resistance to attacks. At the plain of Mars—difficulties, especially at the start, discouragement, black thoughts. At the mount of the Moon—good fortune by chance or by other people.

Stopping at the head line: Rash act or brain trouble At the heart line—heart trouble or change of position owing to an affair of the heart. At the mount of Saturn—happy old age. If forked, difficult old age.

If cut on Saturn by cross lines—obstacles, misfortunes. Rising towards the middle finger—great destiny for good or for evil. Rising towards Jupiter—success.

Very red, possibility of catastrophes.

Lengthened across the lines of the wrist—tragic destiny.

. . . . . .

The Line of Sun.—This line rises from various points of the hand, but most frequently from the ring round the wrist or the head or heart line towards the root of the ring finger where the mount of the Sun is, which it dents with a more or less pronounced groove. It shows the enthusiasm of the being (for the Sun means expansion) and it is very lucky. He who has it well marked may expect renown. It is in short the true line of luck. He in whom it is lacking may fear that he will never succeed. *All chosen people or those who have arrived possess it.*

For the division of the ages we count 30 (from the bottom) up to the head line, 40 to the crossing with the heart line. The Sun line does not generally start before the head or the heart line, because it is towards the age of 30 that the future unfolds itself.

Starting from the heart line, if the solar furrow runs beautifully towards the mount by the ring finger it indicates talent, success, nobility of soul (Sully-Prudhomme, Séverine). If from the head line—the will to arrive by means of the arts or literature (Gyp). If from the intuition line—good qualities which are somewhat spoilt by excessive imagination. From the line of Saturn—success and intellectual fame (the elder Dumas, Gounod, Déjazet). From the mount of Venus or the life line—brilliant omen (Meissonnier, Victor Hugo, Marcelin Berthelot). From the mount of the Moon—success for poets, artists, comedians. From the plain of Mars—agitated fighting, success through struggle (Rodin, Réjane, Clémenceau). From the mount of Mars, it excites to ambition, daring (Got, the younger Dumas, F. Labori, Sarah Bernhardt).

Doubled or tripled—great reputation (Lamartine, Aubert, Corot).

If the solar line ends at Mercury, love of money; if on Saturn—missed vocation.

Crossed by small lines—obstacles (the painter Diaz).

The Line of Intuition runs to the mount of Mercury, starting from the life, fate or sun line. Clean, long, regular, it means good health, good memory, eloquence, intuition. Its appearance as in all other lines indicates the intensity of these qualities.

The Hepatic (or health) *Line* goes from the mount of Venus to the line of Life. H. Rem denies the tradition concerning it, declares that its traditional qualities are very doubtful, and says that further it is often mixed up with the mercurian line.

. . . . . .

Other lines and signs in the hand :—

The Ring of Venus.—Half circle surrounding the middle and ring fingers. The ancient chirologists called it a sign of violent passion, of lasciviousness. H. Rem believes in this sign only if it is double, triple, badly drawn, broken. Otherwise it is merely a sign of increased vitality, increased fortune.

The Lascivious Line.—This line, sister of the intuition line, resembling the milky way, made of all kinds of little parallel lines, seems to betoken excessive ardour in love, voluptuousness.

THE OCCULT SCIENCES

Rings Round the Wrist.—These are small lines which form a kind of bracelet round the wrist. There are two or three, rarely more. It is said that each denotes 30 years of life. But certain reservations must be made on this subject. The data of the line of life are sufficient and more sure. Let us confine ourselves to the following notes :—

Badly marked, much interrupted—not very good health, long illnesses.

Short—accidents which may prove fatal.

Single—bad health and short life.

But it may be that towards the age of twenty these lines become more numerous, deeper, longer. Therefore let us not make this prediction unless we know more.

Quadrangle.—This is the rectangular space, also called the Table of the hand, situate between the heart and head lines.

A regular spacious quadrangle indicates balance, loyalty, benevolence. If it is missing in one hand it is a bad sign. If it is narrow it betokens irresolution, lack of go, of spontaneity, and this omen is strengthened if there are many small lines in it.

Great Triangle.—Formed by the head, heart and intuition lines in the inside of the hand. Well marked it indicates mental balance. The contrary indicates opposite qualities. If narrow it points to narrow-mindedness. If it gets stronger during the course of life, it means that the latter improves.

Small Triangle.—The meeting of the hepatic (or intuition) line with the heart and fate lines. Well formed it denotes a taste for the liberal professions. Archeologists and collectors have it strongly marked.

. . . . . .

A fairly considerable number of small signs further occur in the graphic of the hands, and further interpret the lines and the mounts. They are as follows with their meanings according to their position :—

Stars.—Desbarolles says that they announce inescapable events deriving from the place they occupy. According to H. Rem the following list may be drawn up :—

A star on Jupiter—success, wealth; on Saturn (always bad) paralysis, disastrous death; on the Sun, wealth not bringing happiness, perils; on Mercury, unscrupulousness; on Mars, serious wound, death in war; on the Moon, peril from water (shipwreck or otherwise); on Venus, probable disappointments; in the quadrangle, good disposition; on the head line, wound in the head or madness; at the end of the head line—head wound or rash act; on the life line, misfortunes;

CHIROMANCY

on the Sun line—catastrophe if that line is broken; on the ring of Venus, crime of passion, venereal disease.

On the ring round the wrist—legacy. At the tip of the thumb, excessive gallantry. On the back of the thumb, voluptuousness. On the tip of the fingers—peril.

Crosses.—Sign of minor fatalities (except on the mount of Mercury), especially if well shaped.

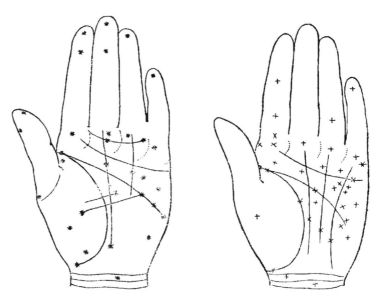

STARS AND CROSSES

Astride on the root of the first finger—happiness; on Jupiter—love marriage; on Saturn—mysticism; on the Sun—missed fame; on Mercury—tendency to theft; on the lunar mount—danger on the water; on the mount of Venus—single and fatal love; in the quadrangle, below the middle finger—mysticism; at the beginning of the life line—accident in childhood; in the life line—unfortunate event; in the middle of the head line—brain trouble; on the heart line—accident; on the Fate line—alteration of position; on the solar line—stoppage of luck; on Mercury—aptitude for science, especially occult science;

THE OCCULT SCIENCES

on the Sun—leaning towards religion (without mysticism); on the ring round the wrist—unexpected wealth.

Dots.—Their colour is as important as their position.

Dark—bad omen; red—trouble with health; white or pink—good sign; red on the heart line—love troubles; white on the same line—sentimental lightheartedness; on the line of fate—obstacles; on the line of life—illnesses or wounds; on the head line—wounds; on the Sun—sorrows; on Saturn—accident very soon; on Mercury—business gone wrong; on the nails—nerves.

Chains.—They indicate a succession of obstacles on the lines—fetters.
On the line of Life—broken health.
On the line of Heart—slight and numerous passions.
On the line of Fate—reverses.
On the line of Fame—bad sign.
On the little finger—confused imagination not very apt at disentangling itself.

Branches.—Leading to the middle finger—effort needed.
Leading to the little finger—practical tendencies.
On the line of Fate—dangers.
On the line of Heart—affection ideal (if rising) or low (if falling).
On the line of Life—health, success, wealth.

Isles.—Two little curves touching at the ends—bad sign.
On the line of Life—clandestine child.
On the line of Heart—adultery.
On the line of Fate—life ruined as the result of adultery.
On the line of Fame—life ruined.
At the base of the little finger—beware of theft and bankruptcy.

Figures.—Approximate figure 5—serious and sad events.
Form of 4 on the mount of Venus—marriage of inclination.

Sign of Venus—(a little circle surmounted by a cross) great love shared.
If the cross is below, this love is the source of sorrow.

Sign of Mars (circle surmounted by an arrow)—strength. Love of fighting. Duels.
On the line of Life—success due to courage or to decision.
On the line of Heart—genesic strength.
On the line of Fate—favourable sudden event.
At the base of the little finger—success due to good policy.

Crescents.—Inconstancy, removals.
On the line of Fame—leanings towards music.
On the ring finger—literary vocation.

CHIROMANCY

Bars.—At the top and close together on the mount of Mercury they indicate in doctors medical intuition (remark of Desbarolles). Horizontal going from the Moon to the outer seam—travels.

Forks.—These are two pointed branches departing from a principal line.

Ascending—good omen. Descending towards the upper part of the hand—reverse in fortune and lack of success in current enterprises.

Rails.—Their name shows to what these signs resemble. If placed on a line they hinder its effect.

Suns.—Circles with rays. At the root of the little finger—success in science; on the ring finger—prediction of fame; in the hollow of the hand—victory over difficulties; at the root of the thumb—gallant successes; on the Moon—journeys.

Squares.—Tokens of energy. If numerous—luck abroad.

Small triangles.—If numerous—abilities.

. . . . . .

We want to draw attention again to the very remarkable work of G. Muchery on the signs, visible in the hand, of heredity, of illnesses and of death which the very learned organiser of the International Congresses of Psychology has observed during years of experiments on hundreds of hands of scholars, of artists, of patients, of madmen, of centenarians, etc.

It is a medical chiromancy into which our scheme does not allow us to go in detail, but which is of the highest interest. We are convinced that in the very near future Medicine will take official note of it, for in the opinion of the author it is possible to discover in the hand very clear symptoms of all kinds of perturbations of the organism, such as poor circulation of the blood, albuminuria, cancer, diabetes, epilepsy, troubles of the stomach, the kidneys, the eyes, the legs, the throat, the bowels, gout, hysteria, premature impotence, rheumatism, paralysis, tuberculosis, etc. Also sudden and accidental death, tendency to suicide, madness, and so on.

In the same book a very curious chapter deals with the signs of intellect, and an analysis is given of a great number of eminent people.

X

Seeming Contradictions and Combinations

It may happen that an analysis made with the help of the above details leads to contradictions of predictions. The reason for this will be that observation was defective. Further, certain combinations

THE OCCULT SCIENCES

or junctions of the lines modify their individual significance. And besides no one has a character all of one piece. A man having a certain defect may at certain times show a reaction, a move towards the opposite direction. Let us take one by one the lines of which we have spoken.

Line of Life.—Cleanly separated from the Head line, it denotes a light fantastic individual, not very sure in his dealings, but succeeding by his self-confidence.

If it joins that line between the thumb and the first finger, it denotes on the other hand a well-balanced mind which does not give in to fancies.

If the three lines (life, head and heart) join, beware of fancies. These people are not very much masters of themselves. They must beware of accidents and catastrophes.

The line of Life interrupted by small lines indicates that the liver must be looked after.

If the lines of Life, Heart and Head form a square well designed, it is a token of an equable character and a good constitution.

If the mount of Venus extends as far as Jupiter, it is a sign of violent passions, and sometimes of sudden death.

Line of Heart.—If mixed up with the Head line—tendency to a " thunderclap " in love.

If the join is towards the middle of the palm—disappointments in love may cause violent actions.

If the Heart line surrounds Mercury up to the folding of the hand—self-interest pursued in sentimental affairs—infidelity.

Line of Heart descending towards the line of Head—leaning towards platonic love.

Line of Heart ending in a curve towards the root of the first finger—exaggerated mysticism.

Line of Heart traversing the whole hand cutting through the mounts —inconstant feelings.

Line of Heart very near to the line of Head—hypocrisy.

Line of Fate.—Very straight from the ring round the wrist to Saturn, touching the line of Life—existence without troubles, health and wealth.

Mixed up with the line of Life—found in those who have risen through their own merit.

Joined to the small line which traverses the mount of the Moon—variations of fortune due to variations of temperament.

Joined to the line of the Sun—success in the arts.

Starting obliquely from the mount of the Moon—fate upset by dreams.

CHIROMANCY

Starting from the mount of Venus—love will be the great preoccupation of life.

Ending in a cross towards the mount of the Sun—mental derangement through crashing of expectations.

Ending before the mount of Saturn—melancholy due to lack of mental balance.

Ring of Venus.—Joined to the Line of Heart—risk of stupid acts owing to base love.

Touching the line of the Sun—propensity to voluptuousness.

Line of the Sun.—Joined to the line of Mercury—abilities thwarted by excess of imagination.

Ending at the line of Mercury—eloquence useful in good things.

Directed towards Mars by crossing Mercury—low æstheticism.

Directed towards the mount of the Moon—tendency towards mystic or baroque art.

Mixed up with the lines of Life and of Mercury—sane, balanced and profitable art.

Mounts of the Sun and of Mars mixed up—low art imposing itself by bluff.

Line of Mercury.—Traversing the Head line—sure judgment.

Traversing the Heart line—feeling dominating the practical side.

Ending on the mount of the Moon—characteristic of inventors without the means for action.

Ending on Mercury—practical intellect.

Joining the life line—sign of preparations a long way ahead.

Ending on the mount of the Sun—inventive imagination.

The mounts of Mercury and of Mars joined—laborious and practical temperament.

XI

Luck, Adultery and the Hand

According to Papus [1] :—

A spatulate finger denotes luck in material enterprises.
A square finger denotes luck in scientific enterprises.
A pointed finger indicates luck in art and diplomacy.
Fine lines under the little finger denote aptitude for great commercial affairs.
A fork below the ring finger denotes the probability of becoming rich.
A cross below the first finger (mount of Jupiter)—sign of luck in love.

[1] *The Book of Luck.*

THE OCCULT SCIENCES

If you put your left hand flat on a sheet of white paper so as to see its colour properly, conclude as follows :—

A hand with frankly white ground—luck in business.
A hand of brown colour—luck in daring enterprises.
A hand of red colour —luck in politics.
A hand of yellowish colour—luck in art.

Mr. Georges Muchery on the other hand has written a most curious little book [1] from which we gather the following details which are but an application of chirological ideas to a given psychological case :—

1. When the palm of the hand is more important than the fingers, the owner has more material tastes ; if it is less so, his tastes are more idealistic or intellectual. Therefore, if adultery is committed, according to the hands it will be either sensual or mental (betrayal of the heart rather than of the flesh).

2. The characteristics described above according to the shape of the hands and the fingers, according to the mounts and the lines, adjust their indications, in the case of adultery, to the kind of adultery in question. For instance—distrust in love, says Mr. Muchery, those people in whose hand a line goes from the line of Life to the little finger, especially if the line of Life is tortuous ; you will be deceived all through your life by these people who will play at love whilst thinking only of their own interest. Study well the line of Heart, which denotes the nature and the strength of the affections. If confused and like a chain, it denotes numerous and inconstant love affairs. If connected with the Head line then love is governed by the brain, therefore less frank, less free than in the opposite case. Forks below the first finger and ending the line are a happy omen.

3. Among the signs of the hand relating to adultery must be noticed :—

An isle in the line of Fate or (and sometimes in addition) in the line of the Sun.

A cross on the mount of Venus on the other hand usually denotes one love only.

4. The lines of union (on the flat of the hand, by the little finger) denote by their number the number of free or legal unions in a life, and by their length the duration of such unions.

Chains in these lines of union are a sign of infidelity.

An isle means union with a relative, and sometimes even incest.

Thus a line of union with an isle and joining the ring of Venus which was broken (sign of licentiousness) and, in addition, an isle in the line of Fate informed the author (to whom it was admitted) that

[1] *Conjugal Happiness. Adultery Unveiled to all by the Hand* (Astrale, publisher).

CHIROMANCY

the man in question, married to a widow, had as his mistress a daughter of the latter.

5. Taking the indications of the mounts into consideration, Mr. Muchery gives the following advice :—

Young ladies, choose a husband who has :—
A large thumb (sign of activity—he will always be able to earn your bread).
A single line of union.
None of the signs of adultery.
A hand a little thick (success) with long and smooth fingers (patience, preciseness).

If you are sensual :—
A long and good line of Heart.
A thick and firm mount of Venus.
A simple ring of Venus.
Coloured lines.

If you are sentimental rather than sensual :—
A long and somewhat soft hand.
A long and straight line of Head.
A straight and plain line of Heart.
A low and soft mount of Venus.

If you want to rule him :—
A small thumb.
A short Head line.
Smooth and square fingers.

Signs of jealousy :—Ball shaped thumb. Heart line going from Mars between the first and middle fingers.

Signs of kindness :—Heart line long, straight, without chain or breaks.

Constancy is never found in a man who has at the same time :—
A chain-like Heart line.
A ring of Venus.
A small Head line.

. . . . . .

Following up these general data, Mr. Muchery gives the prints of a certain number of types of hands of adulterers, from which we select the following :—

1. *Type of unfaithful hand :*—Numerous lines. Ring of Venus well defined. Heart line too long. Mount of Venus too large and not high enough. First finger pointed (curiosity). Isle of adultery on the line of Fate.

2. *Type of hand of adulterous and jealous woman :*—Deep and strong lines. Thumb ball-shaped (changeable temper). A line goes from Venus, divides, forms an isle and ends at the Head line :—this shows that the death of a person who was loved was followed by neurasthenia

in the subject, and by a fresh love. Another line goes from the Life line, crosses the plain of Mars and ends at Mercury—towards the age of 30 a fresh liaison without giving up the first (isle in the Saturn line), hence adultery.

3. *Type of hand of woman born to deceive men :*—Head line forked (lies and cunning in getting out of all difficulties). Mount of Venus high and broad (sensual passion). Line of adultery giving rise to two others going towards Mercury and the Sun (practical use of her lovers).

4. *Type of adultery without knowing it :*—Short, broad, firm, material hand. Head line straight (frankness). Mount of Venus lined (solid appetites). No line of adultery. This woman had a lover of whom she did not know that he was married.

5. *Type of adulterous man succeeding through women :*—Sign of unhappy marriage—Heart line joining the Life line and forming a cross on Jupiter. Sign of the divorce which followed :—line starting from Venus, crossing the Life line and joining the Head line by a cross. Sign of a liaison which brought him money in the line of the Sun. Sign of licentiousness—double ring of Venus.

XII

A Specimen Print

As a practical conclusion of this chapter we give here the photograph of a print of a hand made by Mr. Muchery who will himself in a short analysis tell us what he thinks of it :—

Hand signed by the Moon and Mars, hence hand of an active and imaginative type giving for this reason contradictions or rather a succession of selenian and martian impulses which may also at times be combined.

This imagination of the subject will not be sterile dreaming, as Mars will always try to carry it into effect; but actions are sometimes precipitate, whilst certain periods are calm, even taciturn and melancholy. The subject will have to pass through crises of pessimism, even neurasthenia, but there is the probability that his discouragements will not last long and will be followed by fresh flashes of effort and enthusiasm.

By its shape the hand is artistic and sensual, denoting the taste for the beautiful and the good. Whether he holds a pen or a brush, the subject will do strong æsthetic work which will be surrounded by charming details, for the influence of the Moon will soften everything he touches.

CHIROMANCY

Intellect mixed, at once synthetic and analytic, fond of details and also of the whole, judging sanely and without spite when he becomes critical. Square hand, ruling in spite of the Martian influence.

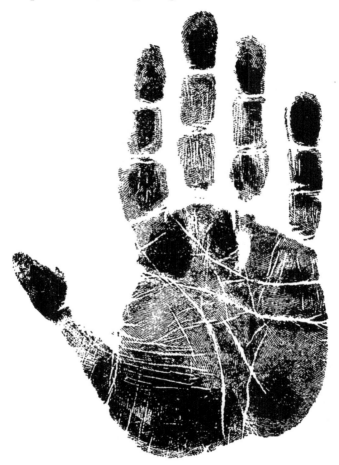

The health does not seem very strong, but has improved, for physical resistance is written on a good little mount of Venus.

The Head line is remarkable—strong mental activity and great sensitiveness come through the branches from the heart rather than

THE OCCULT SCIENCES

the brain; patience for a task of long duration, and constant desire to learn (first finger pointed, sign of intellectual curiosity).

Good Heart line denoting goodness, sensitiveness, impulsiveness, and also defective circulation of the blood (forks, bars on Mars which may cause hemoptysis). Bars on Saturn and vertical lines crossing the Heart line—weakness of the legs to be feared in the future.

Nails short (critical sense). The hand of a man gifted for medicine (in which he would certainly have succeeded). But also the hand of a writer (some of the fingers spatulate). Result ability for documentary work.

Union of the lines of the Heart and the Head—timidity, lack of self-confidence, physical crisis towards the 20th year, which will recur towards the age of 55 under the shape of a loss of vitality which, however, may be avoided by preventive means.

On the whole a good hand of slow, difficult, but certain ascent (on account of the existence of a line of the Sun).

. . . And now may we say that this hand, giving *correctly in every detail* the above psycho-medical portrait, is that of the writer of our Introduction. We assert that the young and famous chiromancer had never before seen the writer of the introduction to this Encyclopædia. Those who know him as poet, essayist and novelist will be surprised at such a correctness down to the smallest details.

We should therefore like to see, as was done at the third International Congress of Experimental Psychology (1923), of which Mr. Muchery himself was one of the organisers, that Chirology should be applied by heads of institutions and by doctors, for it would in the most interesting manner give them information about the persons committed to their care.

Printed in Great Britain
by Amazon